GROW RICH

Title: Grow Rich

Author: Kambiz Mostofizade

Publisher: Mikazuki Publishing House

ISBN-13: 978-1-942825-43-2

Grow Rich is the continuation of the Secrets of Making Money, which teaches you the secrets of Bankers and Rich Investors. Learn the secrets of making money and change your life permanently.

GROW RICH

Introduction

You can sit around and complain about people getting rich around you or you can do something about it. You can change your life. Think about your days. Time keeps moving whether you want it to or not. You are sitting and dreaming about the life you should have without the proper roadmap to guide you there. You may think that you are not ready but if you are reading this then you are ready to take the next step in your life. There are no limitations to what you can achieve as long as you are willing to attempt to achieve them. You deserve to have a yacht and you deserve to drive a new sports car. The question is, are you willing to take the steps to make it happen? The first thing that you have to do is to take initiative and to accept

GROW RICH

responsibility for your own life. You are the master of your own destiny. Forget your past mistakes, forget past relationships that went wrong, and focus on what you can achieve in your life today. Your first goal should be to make one million dollars. If you cannot make one million dollars then you will not be able to make one billion dollars. There are many roads to achieving this goal but it is important that you understand all the roads that lead to success. If you want to get rich and stay rich then you must have a system in place to do so. This system must be capable of generating revenue for you in your sleep. Passive income generates money while you sleep. This book is based around the various ways that you can generate passive income and the

GROW RICH

opportunities that are available for you to reach success.

Patience and hard work lead to success.

Money Has Rules

1. Never invest in a business or financial vehicle that you do not directly control. If the ship sinks and in business it often does, you will be angry and you will play the blame game. If the business wins, you will win. If the business fails, there is a lack of accountability and your investment disappears.

GROW RICH

2. Never make an un-collateralized loan. If someone wants to borrow money from you, then they must present some form of collateral that is financially viable. If someone wants to borrow money from you then they should provide something of value that you could sell to recover your money.

3. Gold has been a traditionally safe investment that has risen in value steadily over the past 100 years. There is a reason why all Central Banks of every nation on earth invest their money in Gold bullion. Gold cannot be reproduced in contrast to paper money which can be printed. Gold is scarce and valuable. The

GROW RICH

price of Gold is uniform and it is a tradable commodity.

4. Real Estate has been a traditionally safe investment that has risen in value steadily over the past 100 years. Most people that are millionaires became so through the acquisition and sale of real estate.

5. Investing in a business you will start and operate is great and adventurous. Just understand that 90 percent of startup businesses fail in the first year.

6. Money loses value over time which is why money is invested in

GROW RICH

financial vehicles that have
higher and higher rates of return.

7. Friendship and business are two
   different things. Don't ruin
   friendship in order to force
   businesses to start.

8. Money is not an end to itself.
   Money is a means to provide
   safety, security, and happiness.

9. Money should be never be
   trapped in low producing financial
   vehicles.

10. There is no logic that could
    provide financial predictions. All
    investments are speculations.

GROW RICH

The Mindset

The first rule of money is never lose control of your money. No one can make a decision for you better than you can. If you hand your money over to someone else, they will decide for you. It is your money and it is your right to decide what you want to do with it. If you decide to spend it on an investment then that is your choice. It is up to you to make informed decisions. The first decision you must make is never lose control of your money. Once you lose control of your money, it is expensive and difficult to get it back. It takes a long time to recover from financial loss. It takes a long time to bounce back after setbacks or defeat. You will only prolong the length of your recovery by trusting your money to others. Make your own

GROW RICH

informed investment decisions and you will see the benefits of your actions. Negative people have a way of bringing others down to their level. They want others to also feel negative and depressed just because they are negative and depressed. What they need is motivation and they need the will to win. You can't be micro-managed on the way to success. If you become successful you can only thank yourself and if you fail you can only blame yourself. If you want to succeed you have to learn to remove negative and toxic people from your life. You should not have your ambitions crushed because someone else is un-easy with your drive for success. If you want to become a success, you have to avoid negative and toxic people, simply because their negativity and toxicity is

GROW RICH

contagious. They have the mindset that nothing should be tried because you could fail. Because they have never done anything they fear that you will actually do something and become successful at it. They want you to do nothing so that they can have the satisfaction they are right and you are wrong. Anything you propose to them is wrong because they have a negative and toxic attitude towards growth. They want to play it safe and playing it safe means doing absolutely nothing will the clock keeps ticking away. How many ticks do you think you have before your clock stops ticking? No one can tell you that with certainty, but the one certainty that we all do face is that of time. Time is finite and fleeting. Time is not on your side unless you are invested in progress. Doing nothing does not make

GROW RICH

the rest of the world stop doing
something. Doing nothing is actually
more dangerous and risky than doing
something. Do you think the prices of
real estate or gold or other assets stop
rising just because you have decided to
do nothing and to wait and see what
happens. I will tell you what happens.
Time just keeps going and the prices of
everything on earth keep rising. That is
what happens. It is called inflation and it
is a reality anywhere on earth. As new
money is generated by everyone on
earth, you are sitting and doing nothing.
The price of real estate and gold and
other assets keep rising to beat inflation
and that means life gets more expensive
for you every year. Over the past 100
years, real estate prices have safely and
steadily risen. Everything keeps rising in
price as the value of your money

GROW RICH

decreases. A 5 bedroom house in Los Angeles had a price tag of $300,000 in 2000. What is the price of that home today? $1,500,000. That is a 5 times (500%) increase in 20 years. A 2 bedroom apartment in Las Vegas had a price tag of $50,000 in 2015. What is the price of that home today? $150,000. That is a 3 times increase (300%) in 5 years. Do you have more buying power today in comparison to 5 years ago? No. The price of food, gasoline, as well as utilities have increased. The overall cost of living has increased in major and minor cities. As the price of real estate and gold increase, retail shops and wholesalers raise their prices to not fall behind. Soon, everyone is raising prices on everything so they do not fall behind. This causes the prices of everything to rise and to lower your quality of life.

GROW RICH

Doing nothing will not make you rich and there are many signs that it could make you poor in the future. If you do nothing, then you have gained nothing, but you doing nothing has absolutely no effect on the prices of real estate and gold rising. They will continue rising whether you do something or if you do nothing. This is why it is so important to move your money in to investments that can at least beat the rate of inflation. If you don't, then your money will be of less value next year in comparison to this year. This is an un-changeable reality that has to be understood and accordingly adjusted to. You have to keep finding new vehicles (real estate or business or gold) that will provide you with a rate of return that is higher than that of the rate of inflation. Inflation is most certainly caused by an increase in

GROW RICH

the money supply. If everyone on earth is investing or working and generating new money, do you think the increase in money supply will raise or lower the value of your money? It will most certainly lower the value of your money which is why your money is not worth the same amount next year. While you are doing nothing to stay completely safe from loss, the value of your money lowers and this also has an effect on the rise of real estate prices (and other assets as well). Business cannot be avoided for the sake of safety. Business has to be embraced for the sake of future security. If the business successful, it will open many new doors for you in other investment avenues. If it fails, then it was a learning experience for you. Let us say that you try something new in business and you do

GROW RICH

fail. Did the world end? Did you die? Is your reputation tarnished? No. You learned from it and gained real world business experience. Business experience is either learned from others or it is learned firsthand. It costs money to gain that knowledge regarding the vast world of business. You can acquire that knowledge from fortune-tellers and you cannot acquire that knowledge by thinking about it. Business experience costs money and time. Business experience took effort to be gained. If you don't do business, how will you learn it? In any given business investment, a myriad of problems could arise. Do you quit at the first sign of trouble? If you do, then you may not be a good business investor. A business investor has to be willing to weather the storm and accept the current difficulties

GROW RICH

and move past them in order to get to the future rewards. It is difficult to bear complex situations that last for periods of time. You have to be thick-skinned in business and be able to take two steps back in order to take one step forward. Every angel investor or venture capitalist has faced difficult, hardship, and setbacks from their various business investments. If it were easy, then everyone would be rich.

What I Learned From Getty

1. Getty believed that overhead costs are a lie and a scam, used only as cosmetic dressing to project an image of success. Getty signed all his oil contracts on the hood of his "Tin Lizzie" aka Model-T Ford. At the height of Getty's wealth, all his

GROW RICH

international oil ventures that
generated tens of billions of
dollars were run from a modest 5
story building that held no more
than 100 people.

2. You cannot expect your
employees to work harder than
you. If you tell your employee to
show up at 7:30am, you better be
there at 7am. Getty having
himself worked as a roughneck
on an oil rig, believed in leading
from the front, not barking orders
from the back.

3. Do not invest in a business
that you cannot directly control.
Better yet, the best business
according to Getty is the

GROW RICH

business that you control, but own no stake in.

4. A sophisticated man is a man that loves art, theater, and music. Getty believed that the downfall of society (the creation of the un-sophisticated person) stems from its lack of appreciation for art.

5. Employees should be rewarded according to performance (bonuses) and their annual salary should be adjusted to reflect the company's strong or weak performance.

GROW RICH

What I Learned From Hershey

The frugal Dutchman went bankrupt 7 times before becoming a success but he never gave up his determination to win. His success wasn't Hershey chocolate as that came after his success with selling caramels for a penny a piece. His success with caramels funded Hershey Chocolate Bars that were priced at a nickel in the early 1900's. His success from his caramels funded the construction and development of a rural township in to a city called Hershey, Pennsylvania. Before he was 60 years old, he gave away ALL his riches to a Trust that still exists today. This Trust created the Hershey School that funds thousands of students every year from around the U.S. Having lost his Irish-American wife Kitty to illness and not having children inspired Hershey to

19

GROW RICH

create the Hershey School. These students live in Hershey, Pennsylvania at the school dorms, receiving a first rate education at the expense of the Hershey Trust. In fact, it is this Trust that controls the Hershey company, not the other way around.

Hershey's life taught me:

1. Success has no monetary figure. Success is about achieving not about earning money. Hershey kept achieving despite his many setbacks and failures and this eventually lead to his success. Do not be put off by failure. It is a part of success.

2. You must risk all to win all. If you want to win you have to be 100% determined to win with every

GROW RICH

available resource at your disposable. Hershey invested nearly everything he had in the creation of Hershey, Pennsylvania and was rewarded greatly for his vision.

3. Sales volume is more important than high profit margins. Hershey chocolates consistently sold because they offered more chocolate in their bars at a lower price than their competitors.

4. Money should be used for greater purposes than self-indulgence. Hershey gave away nearly everything he had before the age of 60. He did this to fund the Hershey School that provided a

GROW RICH

first class education to thousands from across the U.S.

5. You have to know as much or more than your employees. Hershey was a hands-on leader and spent much of his time experimenting to create new milk chocolate bars and confectionaries.

Everyone is not able to bear the arduous road of business and everyone is not suited for being a business investor. Self-help critics love to point out the failures without pointing out the successes. There are many more failures than there are successes in business and that is a common trend in every business on earth. If you wake up in the morning and you have no drive to

GROW RICH

succeed, then you should go back to sleep. The bed is for rest. Once you wake up, you need to be motivated to win and motivated to achieve success. You can't sleep your problems away and you can't sleep yourself to money. It has never worked for anyone. You have to face the harsh and brutal reality of life and that is that it runs on money. If Americans are overly money seeking, it is because they are overly extended in their expenditures. Expenditures can only be reduced to a point before completely eroding your quality of life. You have to live somewhere and you will need means of transportation. These are basic understandings. But sleeping your problems away will never make them go away and it certainly won't make you rich in any way. You have to fight for your future. Everyone

GROW RICH

fights for their future and for their success. You have to do the same. Whether if you are a billionaire reading this book or if you are broke and homeless, you both have the same chances at success. What you are learning in this book, the millionaire and billionaire already know. You both have access to the Internet, you both have access to a phone (hopefully), you both have access to some means of transportation, and you both are able to only eat one meal at a time. You are not lacking anything. If you have the will to win, your period of hardship and difficulty will pass, and you will be able to look back on your time in difficulty and laugh about it. Whether if it takes you one or two or three years, you can climb out of your current situation and emerge as a winner. You have to be

GROW RICH

willing to take the steps to achieve success and that means you have to take your hardship and turn it in to motivation that will fuel your growth. Growing pains are the difficulties we face when we are progressing. It is natural to face multiple problems. This is completely reasonable and natural. It is not natural for you to lay down and quit or to give up in the face of difficulty. That is not acceptable whatsoever. You have to take your difficulties and to channel them in to your drive for success. Self pity has never made anyone rich. Negativity is self-assuring pity and it plays on our innate need to be validated even in loss. The only validation you need is that of your own. You cannot seek others to validate your drive for success. Everyone has excuses for why they didn't try doing business but you

GROW RICH

rarely hear about the reasons why you should be doing business. Do you want to own a house? Do you want to feel successful? Then you have to take the steps and make the effort to achieve that success. When you achieve it, you can only thank yourself for it. When you listen to other people's business advice and you fail, then you can only blame other people. The only way to operate in business is to accept full responsibility and this way you can thank yourself when you do achieve success. Unless you try, how will you know if you have what it takes to be a successful investor? The point of this book is not to give you theories. The point of this book is to get you to go out there and make money for yourself, in order to improve your own life (and people you love). Toxic people tend to be contagious in

GROW RICH

their negative attitudes and they act as if everything is impossible. They turn a simple task in a difficult one with their negativity. That is why they are to be avoided. If you look at the track records of people that give you business advice in your own personal life, you will notice that they do not have a successful track record in business. You should take business advice, from people that have actually employed people and operated businesses. Toxic people lack the business background to give you advice and they believe that no business should be done as to avoid risk all together. The truth is that you cannot avoid risk. You can only manage risk. Each investment in a business or even real estate is surely a risk, but if you do your due diligence and choose wisely, you will come to understand that they

GROW RICH

are safe risks. The only way to avoid all risk in business is to never do business. Nothing ventured, nothing gained is a true statement. You have to be courageous and be willing to take risks when it comes to investing in businesses. Every angel investor or venture capitalist, however successful, has lost money at one time or another investing in a business. If someone has never experienced loss in business, then that is dangerous because they will believe that they are unable to lose (creating even bigger losses).

You have to tell yourself the following:

I AM A WINNER THAT WAS BORN TO WIN IN LIFE. I WILL BE SUCCESSFUL.

Naysayers, toxic, and negative people only want to focus on the people that

GROW RICH

failed rather than focusing on people that were successful. It would be just as false to promote an image of business investors winning all the time. No one wins all the time and no one loses all the time. It is not even always, but more often than not, business investing is 50/50. You could win or you could lose. External conditions will determine the outcome of the business in the future and the Profit and Loss Statement will determine the outcome of the business in the short term. It is not anyone's business to decide for you what is right or what is wrong in business investing. It is obviously wise to have specialists such as an accountant and lawyer view the company's papers, but it is ultimately your choice when it comes to preference of one business investment or another. Businesses fail for various

GROW RICH

reasons and they include but are not limited to:

Lack of Demand

Poor Customer Service

Sub-standard Quality

High Price

High Burn Rate

Financial Mis-management

In-consistent Supply Chain

If you understand the reasons a business can fail, you can seek to avoid businesses that have such pitfalls. Sales number would provide you with proof of lack of demand. Poor customer service can be discovered with an email or a phone call. Sub-standard quality of the product can be discovered through by

GROW RICH

viewing it, touching it, and/or comparing it with other products. High price can be discovered by comparing the product with similar products in the marketplace. High burn rate and financial mis-management can be discovered by viewing the Profit and Loss Statement as well as Balance Sheet. An inconsistent supply chain can be fixed by sourcing through multiple suppliers. There are many ways to discover if a business has pitfalls and it is through due diligence that it is done. Not all businesses should be invested in, just as not all real estate should be bought. You have to discriminate between buying one real estate property or another. In investing in a business, you have to have the same level of discrimination to be able to choose between one business investment or

GROW RICH

another. I know of a tech venture capitalist that was able to make a lot of small investments in various tech companies that were ultimately sold to major tech companies. He did really well and was able to attract global investment for his VC funded tech start-ups. Did he fail at all? Of course he did as do all humans that are seeking to be successful in the world of business. You win some, you lose some, but you keep moving forward in business. That is how the game is played. Crawling under a rock and soaking in a pool of self-pity won't make you any money. You have to tell yourself the following:

I AM A WINNER THAT WAS BORN TO WIN IN LIFE. I WILL BE SUCCESSFUL.

Repeat the above sentence 100 times. Time is your friend and you have to

GROW RICH

make use of time by not wasting it on frivolous activities. You have to focus on achieving success, no matter how many setbacks you experience in your personal and business life. Success is not handed to you rather that success is earned through hard work and focused efforts. Anyone that received anything on a silver platter, ended up not being able to make money so they had to sell the silver platter. Once you are an experienced and savvy business and real estate investor, you will be the one holding all the silver platters. You will be able to buy gifts for your friends and family, you will be able to buy the home you always wanted, you will not be ashamed of having things that you deserve, and you will be a happier and more productive member of society. Money changes lives and it can and will

GROW RICH

change your life permanently. You have to be pro-active and bring in the money as the money will not chase you. You have to chase your dreams and money is an effect of your activities. No one can be you and that is your super-human power in life. You have to choose success and choose to be around others that are involved in chasing success or have found success. You have to believe in yourself when no one else does. You have to believe in what you want to accomplish. You have to believe that you can be successful and you have to believe that you deserve success. There are thousands of ways to get rich and they include investing in businesses, investing in gold, investing in stocks, and investing in real estate. The vast majority of millionaires became rich through real estate. Real estate is

GROW RICH

not easy to get rich off. There is nothing that is easy in life or in anything. Anything that is achieved is done so by hard work and long hours of dedication. Get rich schemes are more likely than not Ponzi schemes or pyramid schemes. Real Estate is not digital coin you can't touch or feel. You can touch real estate and you can repair and upgrade real estate. Real estate will increase in value over time while you are sleeping. Real Estate will, over 100 years, increase in value and it will make you rich over 30 years. You will not get rich overnight but you will get rich over 30 years. The sooner you start on your journey the sooner you will be on the road to riches but you will not get anywhere by brooding in a pool of pity and doing nothing. Everyone has had setbacks, delays, losses, and

GROW RICH

heartbreaks. You have to use your setbacks as fuel for your internal drive. You have to take your will and drive to succeed and apply it to the real world. You cannot be afraid of being successful. Buying real estate using owner financing is nothing new and it has been done by tens of thousands of people in the past 10 years. It is the knowledge of what to do with the drive to make it happen that makes what you are learning worth it. You have to be willing to go and see properties from up close and to judge them in a standard way. You have to understand what the signs are that makes a property valuable rather than a money pit. You have to have good taste and good judgment and the ability to choose between hundreds of properties you find. You have to a Success driven

GROW RICH

mindset that powers you forward in the face of uncertainty and various issues that need to be resolved.

Read the next sentence out loud.

I DESERVE SUCCESS AND I AM GOING TO BE SUCCESSFUL

You will earn in life what you work for and you have to work smart and frugal. No one has to believe in what you are doing as long as you believe that you are going to be successful. You have to have the mindset that you are holding a flashlight in the dark and you are leading the path to success. You are trailblazing and creating your own path to success by taking the necessary to achieve it. Naysayers, negative, and toxic people should be avoided at all costs. Since they do not want to take the necessary

GROW RICH

steps to achieve success they attempt to convince others that they can never have it. No one is the master of your destiny but you. Once you make the conscious decision to become successful and to become rich, your mind has a way of adjusting your perception and reality to achieve it.

Read the next sentence out loud.

I DESERVE SUCCESS AND I AM GOING TO BE SUCCESSFUL

Your mind is the most powerful weapon you have and it can make you become successful. Not by thinking about it, but by doing it. By putting in the hours needed to find the right properties to buy, doing your due diligence in order to make sure there are no pitfalls or negatives attached to the sale, placing

GROW RICH

multiple offers on multiple properties, correctly doing the legal paperwork with the help of a Real Estate Lawyer, fixing up the property (cosmetic and structural), renting out the property to a qualified renter, and re-financing the property. It is easier said than done but so are many things worth achieving in life. They take time and effort in order to be achieved. Get rich fast schemes don't work but get rich slow schemes do work and have proven themselves to work. If you are willing to put in the time, you will see the results. Everyone gets jealous when viewing someone else get rich without acknowledging the difficult and time involved to get rich. It is easy to judge others but difficult to be honest with ourselves. If you want to get rich, then you have to take the steps to get you rich. You have to put in the time to

GROW RICH

make you rich. If you want a salary, then get a job. If you want to get rich through real estate, then you have to be willing to be energetic and focused on achieving the success you have envisioned. You deserve the best in life. You deserve to own a home and own a car and own a boat. It takes effort on your part to realize it and it takes time to bring it to fruition. If you use your time wisely and manage your time, you can find properties and visit them. You can analyze and compare properties and make offers on them. You can find lenders that will re-finance them. But it is going to take you being motivated. Read the next sentence out loud.

I DESERVE SUCCESS AND I AM GOING TO BE SUCCESSFUL

GROW RICH

Yes you do deserve success. Not everyone will be successful because not everyone is willing to put in the effort it takes to become successful. Your mindset has to be focused around your success without you becoming sidetracked on new adventures that will take up your time. Do one thing and do that one thing very well. A master of all trades is a master of none. You have to keep doing it until you are both confident in your abilities as well as being familiar with the owner financing sales process. Avoid toxic people that say you can't do it. What they are really telling you is that they can't do it. You can do anything you want as long as you put your mind to it. You can achieve any level of success that you can dream of as long as you are willing to work for it. You have to be strong on the inside as well

GROW RICH

as on the outside. You have to be thick skinned and focused on completing property deals. There are no shortcuts and no easy routes to success. As long as the steps are followed, everyone can be successful using this system. Owner financing real estate is not new and has been done so many times that it is routine (and mundane). The real estate is not going to jump in to your lap. You have to find it and that means searching anywhere and everywhere you can. You have to be pro-active in order to generate passive income. Let us say that together. You have to be pro-active in order to generate passive income. You have to hunt for the deals so that you have a pool of choices to choose from. The more choices you have the better the property you will find. It all comes down to choice and choosing the

GROW RICH

wrong property can make you liable to various costs that you would not incur had you searched for a wide range of properties. The more choices, the better the choice. Owner financed properties are not always pretty. You are going to search through many properties before you arrive at a few good ones. There are a lot of properties that are not worth investing in because they have serious structural damages that could require tens of thousands of dollars of work. You have to spend the time searching in order to find a wide range of properties that you could entertain investing in. Some of them required minimal cosmetic repairs and some of them require structural repairs. Construction costs rack up fast and are costly. You cannot expect to find a pretty home for a low cost. You are more likely to find a large number of ugly homes that have expenses ranging from past due payments to construction. Owner financed homes must be re-habilitated and re-modeled for maintenance purposes and so that you are able to rent out that property to a renter for a higher price. Spending actual time finding owner financed homes and going through the sales process for the first time will teach you through experience. After your first success, you will feel like you are flying on the clouds. Could this really be possible? Yes. If you were un-aware of owner financed deals then you are not alone. There are hundreds of millions of people that are not aware that they can purchase a home using owner financing. The reason they don't do it is because they have no experience in doing it, so they avoid it all

GROW RICH

together. If you do nothing at all then you have no risk whatsoever. In other words, if you take no risks you are completely safe financially but then you will gain nothing. Nothing ventured, nothing gained was as true as when it was said. You have to be willing to take risks in order to win. Every investment vehicle is a form of speculation. You have no way of 100 percent being guaranteed anything. But if you take the steps that people have taken before successfully, then you will stand to gain from their knowledge and experience. What one person can do another can do, is a true statement. Buying owner financed properties are a standard way of purchasing property for individuals that have bad credit, are over-extended in their credit, are out of work, or have no credit. It is a way for buyers to lift

GROW RICH

themselves out of poverty by owning something that is both valuable and real. Real Estate can be lived in, used as an office, used as collateral for loans, and can be developed (townhouses, condominiums, apartments, houses, stores, etc.). It has real value which is why Banks own it. There are many people that have lost money in real estate as well, but the reason is less benign than you imagine. People that lost money in real estate made bad business decisions that cost them money and years of their life. You never invest more than you can and you never become over-extended. To do so would put your entire portfolio at risk. Spending hundreds of millions or losing hundreds of millions of dollars is a game for the ultra-rich one percent. In reality, most real estate is obtainable through owner

GROW RICH

financing if the down payment and loan terms satisfy the seller. It is up to the buyer to be creative in financing and to find ways to satisfy a seller. If the Seller asks for $20,000 down on a $200,000 house, you can ask for the seller to amortize the down payment in to monthly payments that are manageable. If you had to, you could even make an offer on a home that is higher than other bids, if you are able to amortize the down payment in to monthly payments. Some sellers may appreciate that for various reasons. A homeowner facing pre-foreclosure just might appreciate the offer to buy their home while paying off their delinquent payments. Each seller has their own unique reason for selling and it is frankly none of the buyer's business, why they are selling it. The seller may have a myriad of reasons for

GROW RICH

selling it but as long as they are willing to entertain selling it to you on an owner financed basis, they are then an option that you could use when buying. In the beginning of your journey, start off with lower priced homes, under $50,000. As you gain experience buying owner financed homes you can raise your limit to under $100,000. It is important to keep repeating the process in order to be successful and to Grow Rich. Repetition causes familiarity and allows you to become comfortable enough with the process that you are confident in your abilities. The more confident you become, the larger the deals you will seek to transact. It is important to start from the ground level and work your way up in order to acquire a firm grasp on the fundamentals of purchasing owner financed homes.

GROW RICH

The Process

Find Properties – You should spend most of your time sifting through various websites, newspapers, and media outlets in order to find potential properties for bidding on.

Due Diligence – Visit the property and check for damages (cosmetic and structural) or issues that should be addressed. Have Real Estate Lawyer read your Offer before you make it.

Make an Offer – Offer to buy the property using the "Subject to" clause in the contract.

Sign Contract – Use a Real Estate Lawyer and an Official Notary.

Deed & Title – Have Real Estate put in your name.

GROW RICH

Rehab – Fix up the property in order to prepare it to be rented.

Rent – Rent out the property using comparable properties nearby to establish a fair value for rental prices or use a real estate agent to determine the monthly rental price of your newly acquired real estate.

The Formula

The formula is simple. Buy in to passive income or create new streams of passive income. The easiest way to buy in to passive income is to become an investor. You don't need an MBA from a fancy university to become an investor. You don't need a license or a degree to invest in real estate. You need money, courage, and patience to become successful. Most people fail on the road

GROW RICH

to success and never achieve success. It takes hard work and years of dedication to reach success. Some people just get lucky and find success overnight but that is rare and is the exception rather than the rule. The slow and steady way of becoming rich is safe because it is done in a well-planned manner. Passive income is built up over time rather in an instant and that makes it a stable foundation for growth. Getting rich overnight probably means you will lose everything you have overnight as well. It takes time to create value and to build up momentum that achieves success. If you create multiple channels of revenue, these will build up over time and each will become an Active Revenue Channel (ARC). You have to build up your ARC through patience and hard work but it is the foundation of the

GROW RICH

system that you are learning. The ARC System has the advantage of creating multiple channels of revenue from multiple sources. You create multiple streams of revenue that build up your net worth over time. For example, your first ARC could be your job, your second ARC could be your weekend gig DJ'ing parties, your 3rd ARC could be your off-work investing in stocks, your 4th ARC could be your weekend consulting position for businesses, and so forth. The more Active Revenue Channels you create, the more money you will make. The average millionaire has 7 or more Active Revenue Channels that make them money. It is obviously impossible to take on more Active Revenue Channels than you can manage, but you have to stay focused on the idea that Active Revenue Channels increase your

GROW RICH

profitability. Active Revenue Channels fuel your growth and they allow you to Grow Rich over time. There are many popular forms of Active Revenue Channels and they include Real Estate as well as Stock Market Investing. The merits of Real Estate are well known which is why Real Estate is a preferred investment vehicle for investors seeking safe and steady passive income. Real Estate is

Active Revenue Channels create multiple streams of income for you.

by far the most proven among all investments because it has shown to provide steady growth over a period of 20 years or more. If you are seeking to

GROW RICH

get rich overnight, then this book is not for you. History is filled with adventurers that got rich and lost everything overnight. Gamblers, speculators, and pirates gained everything and lost everything overnight. You don't want it overnight and you shouldn't want it overnight. This book can help you get rich over a period of 20 to 30 years. Active Revenue Channels take time to develop and they take time to harvest. Always remember, an investment that can make you rich overnight can also bankrupt you overnight. Slow and steady growth can be achieved by generating passive income through real estate. Real Estate that generates passive income for you becomes an Active Revenue Channel (ARC). You should seek to build up multiple Active Revenue Channels but the most

GROW RICH

important by far is that of Real Estate. Real Estate has shown, over the past 100 years, that it is a safe investment that provides steady growth in value. This is why real estate is so sought after by individuals as well as Banks. There are various ways to purchase real estate but the way you should be concerned about learning is that of the Owner Financed Property. You could waste weeks and thousands of dollars when dealing with Bank mortgages and appraisals. The best way to purchase property without having to deal with any Bank, is to purchase property directly from its owner using Owner Financing (also known as Seller Financing). Owner Financing allows you to bypass dealing with banks, saving you thousands of dollars and saving you time in the process.

GROW RICH

Always seek Professional Assistance from a Real Estate Lawyer before purchasing.

The process of purchasing real estate without using a bank is relatively easy and much less costly than dealing with a bank mortgage. The first and most important step is spending time to find properties that are relatively in good condition, without encumbrances or liens, and is owned outright by the owner/occupant. You could spend many hours finding homes with a lien on them or with a mortgage, but they are not suitable for pure owner financed deals. The pure owner financed deals that you should pursue should be on real estate without any encumbrances or liens and

GROW RICH

without any mortgage. One of the most
popular ways that owner financed deals
have been executed is through lease
purchase agreements. A lease purchase
agreements allows the renter/buyer to
apply their monthly rent payments
towards buying the real estate property.
It is important to take various things in to
consideration before entering in to such
a transaction. What if the property has a
bank mortgage? If a mortgage currently
exists on the house, then the Bank is
the first in line to get paid should the
house get sold. This can complicate
your agreement with the owner. If you
want to purchase real estate using
owner financing and the real estate has
a current mortgage, then you should
always use a "Subject to" clause in your
contract. You have to put in a "Subject
to" clause in your contract that states

that the mortgage stays in place, you as the new buyer make the monthly payment to the seller (who in turn pays the mortgage company), and the deed and title are put in your name making you the owner. Then you are able to re-finance the property. When the property value goes up, you can also sell it and realize the returns. One of my students was able to use my system to purchase a house in sunny Orlando, Florida, for which he contacted me and thanked me. He was a beginner student and had little or no knowledge about real estate and

Owner Financed Deals save you time and reduce your costs.

knew even less about encumbrances or liens. Using the Grow Rich system that I

GROW RICH

taught him, he was able to confidently and easily negotiate an Owner Financed Deal to purchase a home in Orlando, Florida. Home Ownership is not beyond your grasp. You can own as many homes as you want as long as you are willing to put in the hours to sift through thousands of properties and find the right one. Newspapers, real estate websites, real estate agents, and referrals are all key vehicles for finding you owner financed real estate opportunities. You may not be able to purchase $300,000 house on your first deal. Your first deal may be a $20,000 house or a $50,000 house. You are not geographically locked in to any one particular area which is why you should expand your search for real estate to as many places as possible inside and outside the United States. The more

GROW RICH

options you provide yourself for choice, the easier it will be to choose one real estate property from among the thousands you will view per week. You should be willing to spend 4 hours, on average, per week on finding properties that you can choose from. Let us say for example you spend one entire week searching for real estate properties that are suitable for an owner financed deal. During that week you find 10 properties, you make 4 offers, and 1 offer gets accepted. It is a numbers game but it depends on the thoroughness of your search. It is not about doing it part time or full time (9-5). Your search for real estate that is owner financed should be constant and regular in order for it to yield the proper results. Owner Financing has many advantages over traditional financing and they include provide access to funding that they may not have been able to receive from a bank, reduced closing costs, time saved, no appraisal fees, and negotiable down payments. The disadvantages of buying an owner financed home are usually higher rates of interest on the loan and having to make a Balloon Payment at the end of the loan terms. Loan terms for owner financed properties are usually 5 years after which the Buyer seeks a traditional loan or re-financing. The most important items to take in to consideration are the following:

Down Payment – The down payment is the most important item you will negotiate. If you don't have the down payment that the seller is asking for, you can ask that a portion of the down payment is also owner financed in to monthly payments.

Purchase Price – The purchase price is the total price that the seller is selling the real estate property to the buyer. The purchase price should be negotiated in a way that is financially viable for the buyer. Do not buy a property that is based on pure hope. It has to make financial sense.

Loan Amount – The loan amount is the amount that is owed by the buyer to the seller after the Down Payment has been deducted.

Interest Rate – The interest rate should be negotiated so as to not overpay for a real estate property. It is important to note that Owner Financed Deals are

GROW RICH

known to have higher rates of interest than traditional financing.

Loan Term – The loan term provides the time (the number of monthly payments) that are to be paid by the buyer to the seller.

Amortization Schedule – The monthly payment that will be made according to the Loan Terms (number of monthly payments). A part of the monthly payment goes to paying for the Interest on the Owner Financed Property and a part goes to paying of the loan principal.

Patience and hard work lead to success.

Tax and Insurance – The owner financed deal should state the terms as

GROW RICH

related to yearly taxes and insurance on the real estate property being purchased.

Assignability - It is important to guarantee that the contract that the Buyer signs with the Seller, should be assignable so that the property can be sold at a higher value in the future.

If you as the buyer fail to make the payments to the seller according to the agreed contract, the seller has the right and ability to enter in to foreclosure proceedings. If the buyer fails to make the payments, the seller also keeps the Down Payment paid by the buyer. This is why Owner Financing is so lucrative to a home owner. The home owner faces little risk other than having to enter in to foreclosure. The seller makes a higher return and is usually not

GROW RICH

responsible for repairs (depending on the contract terms).

The point of the Grow Rich system is to buy properties using owner financing, fix up the properties (cosmetic and structural repairs), and rent out the properties. This is the way you create an Active Revenue Channel (ARC). There are many people that will think of buying, fixing, and selling a property. Fix and Flip is the term that they themselves use to describe their activities. You should never sell a property. You should buy properties and hold them for life. You should fix, upgrade, and rent out a property in order to create a new Active Revenue Channel. You can Re-Finance the newly acquired Owner Financed Property using a Mortgage Lender. The money you pull out during the re-

GROW RICH

financing can be used to fix and upgrade the property so that it can attract a higher monthly rent. Each new real estate property you acquire through owner financed deals adds one more Active Revenue Channel, building up your monthly revenue stream. It is so important to continue the cycle until you have built up a portfolio of properties that are generating rental income on a monthly basis. The cash flow will empower your balance sheet and allow you to pay off the owner financed loans. Over time, the value of each property will rise and this will allow you to raise your rents and to use them to borrow against. Owner financing is a loan that allows a buyer to buy new real estate without having to waste their money on appraisals and/or wasting times on complex bank loans. By building up your

GROW RICH

portfolio with multiple Active Revenue Channels, you are able to leverage those properties in order to use them as collateral to buy more expensive (more lucrative) real estate properties. There are various reasons why a Seller finds Owner Financed Deals easier and more attractive versus traditional financing. It is not your responsibility to figure that out. In many cases, the buyer is helping the seller by buying their property through owner financing. There may be various reasons why a homeowner may choose to provide owner financing and avoiding banks is just one of them. The homeowner may be past due and be in pre-foreclosure status. The homeowner may be several months late on payments and would rather make money than lose their equity.

GROW RICH

Human Credit

Just as businesses have a credit and people have a personal credit history, people also have a human credit history. Loans are not always available through Banks and individuals are sometimes the only people that can lend you money for a business or real estate investment. Humans do trust each other if they have familial relations and they do lend large amounts of money to each other without consulting any lender, lending company, or bank. The Human Credit industry may not be an industry in the traditional sense of the term, but it does exist. Cousins lend each other $200,000 at a time without any paperwork or promissory notes being exchanged. Humans provide capital to each other without any intermediary all the time and

GROW RICH

they do not have to even know each
other. P2P Lending or Person to Person
Lending is not new, but it is relatively
new to the online world. P2P Lending
exchanges are intermediaries that
function as a marketplace for loan
seekers and individual lenders. It is
important to build up a track record of
ethical business practices that give you
a good reputation and enhance your
likeability. It is a huge factor that is
underestimated as it assumed that all
lending and financing has been based
on numbers. There are instances of loan
seekers showing up to a Bank and
asking for hundreds of millions of dollars
in loans based on a few press clippings
in major newspapers. If it has worked for
them, then it can work for you. A
positive public image is essential to
business operations and loan seekers

GROW RICH

have used Image Projection (showing yourself in a good way) successfully to attract major investors. There are many instances in which a traditional loan cannot be acquired and it is required to leverage reputation to achieve the results you are seeking. If you have a track record of paying back personal loans and maintaining your personal credit with people you have borrowed money from, they will be willing to loan you larger amounts at a later date. Raising capital person to person becomes easier when you have familial relations with them as well as demonstrating that you are responsible when it comes to paying back their money. Un-ethical business conduct and "burning bridges" results in weakening your network of individuals that can assist you on your path to

GROW RICH

success. Your network can raise your net worth if you are able to build relationships and foster them in a mutually beneficial manner. But that depends on always paying back the person or business you have loaned from.

Consultants

A lawyer is a consultant in regards to legal matters. An accountant is a consultant in regards to financial numbers. They are worth every penny they are paid because they have insight and advanced in-depth knowledge regarding legal and financial matters. You should call a Lawyer and call an Accountant before every business decision. They may see something that you do not. Three heads are better than one. It is better to have a legal opinion

GROW RICH

on a business matter than to face legal proceedings. Lawyers like to joke that life is better lived than litigated, and they are right. A good lawyer is the difference between your success and your defeat. A good lawyer will show you the best way to win with the least path of resistance. An accountant can find discrepancies in the numbers and can give you concrete recommendations that can save you time and money. An accountant can also give you recommendations that will prevent you from making an investment that will result in you losing your money. Lawyers and accountants are specialized in their respective fields and their paid advice can help you progress faster and in a safer manner. A business investment should be viewed and analyzed by both an accountant as well

GROW RICH

as a lawyer. A legal perspective can help shape your business direction as well as protect your investment. Many lawyers are also certified public accountants (CPA), and this gives them greater in-sight and advanced knowledge about both legal and financial matters. It is common sense to do it but many people don't subscribe to common sense. Before you make an investment in real estate or a business, make sure you have both an experienced lawyer and accountant analyze it. You will save yourself a lot of time and money and you will be able to make an informed decision.

Debt Re-negotiation

Banks would rather re-negotiate their debts with customers than lose their customer because of a foreclosure.

GROW RICH

Mortgage debt and Business Loans can be re-negotiated with a Bank and it can be lowered substantially through negotiations. You can contact the bank holding the mortgage note or business loan, and re-negotiate the total amount of the loan as well as its terms (amortization, interest rate, etc.). Banks are opening to negotiating with customers and businesses that are in debt to them because it would be more costly for the customer or business to default on that loan. Debt can be re-negotiated and lowered substantially through a few phone calls and its rate and monthly payments can be lowered through negotiation. Even if your name is not on the mortgage note held by the bank, you can offer to the seller of that property you are buying to have their debt re-negotiated with their bank. A

GROW RICH

mortgage broker, real estate agent, or lawyer, can re-negotiate debt for you and save you time. Debt re-negotiation is a standard practice in finance and it can result in saving you money in the short and long term.

Raising Capital

Raising capital provides you necessary funds for investing in real estate and business.

There are various ways to raise capital for investment and they include:

Friends/Family – People tend to over-look friends and family but they are the easiest persons to talk to about investing with you.

Angel Investors – Angel investors are individuals with a high net worth that are

GROW RICH

seeking to increase their net worth through investing in start-up companies. Angel investors tend to be less experienced than institutional venture capitalists but they are easier to approach (and sometimes to work with!). Angel investors take more risks than venture capitalists and are generally more approachable.

Venture Capitalists – Venture Capitalists are investors tied to a firm of investors. VC companies or VC firms have experienced specialized investors with advanced knowledge in various fields such as tech.

Hard Money Lenders – Hard money lenders used collateral to loan money. Also known as Secured Loans or Collateralized Loans.

GROW RICH

Banks – Banks create business lines of credit for companies and can arrange equipment financing. Banks require business line of credit applicants to have higher levels of credit.

Crowd-funding – Many start-up companies found their first funding through the use of online crowd-funding websites.

Customers – Customers can provide capital through a Pre-Order Sale.

Raising Capital is key to success!

Investing in Gold

Gold has always been a traditional form of money that has been relied on as

GROW RICH

currency by potentates, rulers, monarchs, money lenders, and bankers. Central Banks are the largest buyers of Gold on earth and that is because Gold has real value. If all the mined gold on earth was gathered together and melted down, it would not fill three Olympic sized swimming pools. Gold is a safe investment because it has shown steady growth in value over the past 100 years. In 1990, the price of Gold per ounce was around $400. Thirty years later, in 2020, the price of Gold per ounce was around $2000. That is a fivefold increase in 30 years. That is nearly 17 percent a year return on your investment had you bought an ounce of Gold in 1990. 17 percent a year return is a healthy return on your investment. The annual average return on an investment in real estate is 8 percent a year. Gold is

GROW RICH

a safe investment and it is readily accepted by nearly all nations as a valuable form of currency. Nearly 4 billion years ago the earth was bombarded for a long period of time with meteorites that brought rare precious metals with them such as Gold. Because the earth's surface was for the most part covered in water, the oceans of the earth contain the largest amount of Gold and precious metals. The world's oceans are said to contain one hundred and fifty thousand tons or more of Gold and possibly even larger amounts of other precious metals. The amount of Gold on earth is limited to the means available to produce it. The more that paper money is printed, the less value it has. Gold cannot be printed like paper money and it cannot be

GROW RICH

reproduced (except at prohibitively expensive costs).

Gold In Earth's Crust	
Type	**Parts Per Million**
Sedimentary rocks	.0051
Folded belt region	.0038
Crystalline rocks	0036
Continental crust	.0035
Oceanic crust	.0035
Earth's crust	.0035
Continental shield region	.0034
Sub oceanic region	.0029
Deep oceanic region	.004

Source: Tung and Chi-Lung

It is thought that the entire crust and even the core of the earth, contains vast amounts of untapped Gold waiting to be

GROW RICH

discovered. Gold's rarity is because Gold is not a naturally grown commodity like an orange is. Gold cannot be cloned like plants and even animals can. Gold cannot create more Gold, as the alchemists in the Middle Ages lead potentates to believe. Looking at the chart by Tung and Chi-Lung, the deep oceanic region contains the least Parts Per Million (PPM) but due to the vastness of the world's oceans comprising the majority of the earth, there may be a lack of testing to determine indeed how much the deep oceanic crust contains. From a geological point of view, it is important to note that the entire earth contains Gold. If you are able to take a certain percentage of your monthly earnings and buy Gold, then you will be able to save a large amount of Gold over 5

GROW RICH

years. Let us say for example, your monthly income is $4000 per month. If you are able to buy 10 percent of that amount in Gold per month, say $400 per month, then you will have purchased $4800 worth of Gold in one year. Because the price of Gold has historically gone up steadily for the past 100 years, you can count on Gold being more expensive by the second year of your five year gold buying plan. It is important to stick to buying Gold monthly and to save that Gold in a safe and secure location. After buying Gold for 5, 10, or 20 years, you will have amassed a considerable amount of Gold and you will (hopefully) see the price of Gold rise on a steady basis as it has historically done. Gold is a safe investment which is why the largest central banks on earth hold millions of tons of it.

Growth

The five most important elements for a company's growth are from Equity Momentum, Capturing Marketing Share, Inventuring (in-house venture capital investments), Investing in Businesses (External Venture Capital) and Purchasing Companies (Mergers and Acquisitions). Companies that enter shrinking or low growth markets are not going to gain momentum. It is important to view business trends that are increasing growth or decreasing growth. If you are invested in a business that is operating in a low growth market, then you have to transition away to a higher growth market. It is important to understand your skills in the current market you are operating in versus the skills you have to acquire to operate in the new higher growth market you will be moving in to. If you are buying in to a business by investing as an angel investor or venture capitalist, it is important to buy in to companies that are not competing with your current offerings. You should buy in to companies that offer products or services that are complimentary to your portfolio. When you invest in a business that would be complimentary to your portfolio of business investments, you are able to acquire new customers rather than having to develop new customers through expensive marketing campaigns. Either your business has to create new products, improve the quality of products to raise the price, or you have to acquire new customers. Many

GROW RICH

savvy business investors invest in a business that would be complimentary to their own in order to acquire new customers to sell to. If the market is shifting faster than your business can capitalize on it, then acquiring new customers by investing in a business will allow you to gain momentum and create growth. You either have to create new customers by in-house sales, create new customers through outsourced sales, create new customers through business development, or acquire new customers through investments in complimentary businesses. The entire operations of a business, from human resources to manufacturing to customer service, depend on the ability of a business to achieve sales growth. A shrinking business has a shrinking operating budget as well as a shrinking work-force.

Investing In Business

Acting as an Angel Investor or Venture Capitalist in start-up businesses has many benefits and the most important being the satisfaction that is gained from witnessing its success. The difference between an Angel Investor and a Venture Capitalist is that the Angel Investor operates on their own while a Venture Capitalist is tied to other investors. There are various ways to find start-up companies that are looking for angel investors but the easiest way is to make "Angel Investor" part of your job title. You can have a separate stack of business cards specifically for when you attend business conferences and for when you want to meet start-up

GROW RICH

companies. There are various strategies for investing but it is key to be honest with yourself regarding the level of worry you are willing to handle. Of course, when you make an investment in someone (and their business) you have to be positive about various factors including:

Character – Is the person(s) forthcoming in the numbers of the company (Balance Sheet, Profit and Loss Statement)? A business owner that is dodging key questions about business numbers is a tall tale sign that you should be weary of working with such a business owner. A business owner should be up-front and open about their numbers and should not be defensive.

Brand Protected – Is the brand protected? An Angel Investor (Venture

GROW RICH

Capitalist) wants to see patent or trademark protections. You cannot invest in a business that has not protected its intellectual property.

Sales – Does the company have sales? If the company doesn't have sales, does the company have offers to purchase from customers?

Valuation – Companies falsely advertising themselves at 6 times their value makes Angel Investors and Venture Capitalists turn away. You should be wary of investing in a business that over-values themselves. A fair valuation for a start-up company is 1X their yearly gross revenue. You should look to create synergies between your investments. If you invest in an oil field then you could invest in a gas station to create synergies. Synergies

GROW RICH

add value because they allow one investment to help and assist another investment you have made. Another method for arriving at a proper valuation for a business is by comparing it with other similar businesses.

Share – An angel investor or venture capitalist will seek between 20 to 40 percent (or even a controlling majority share) in order for the investment to be viable for them. As an Angel Investor, you should seek to take a sizeable share of a business for investing in it. A 5 percent investment or 10 percent investment in a start-up is not worth your time and money.

Growth – Angel Investors and Venture Capitalists don't invest in industries that have a small market cap. A large industry that is growing is attractive

GROW RICH

while a small industry or shrinking industry is not worth investing in.

Capable – Is the person responsible for the company capable enough to execute the business plan of the company?

Know-how – Does the person responsible for the company have specialization or advanced knowledge in the industry they will be working in?

Pitfalls – Does the company have other investors that will dilute your investment in the future? Does the company or person have a negative reputation? Does the company have past debts? Are there any issues that could be a problem in the future?

GROW RICH

Investing in business is a process that is methodical.

Attitude - It is nearly impossible to work with someone that has a bad attitude. They are toxic and they ooze it. Their toxic attitudes are contagious to a company and its organization. You should never invest in a business run by people that have a bad attitude.

Focused – You can't invest in a business run by a person that is simultaneously running another company. It will destroy your investment and it will not allow your investment in that company to grow. You want the person(s) and company that you invest in to be completely focused.

GROW RICH

Debt – Does the company have debt and if so, what amount? Is the debt for equipment or for raw materials? Is the debt manageable?

Burn Rate – How much does the company spend per month on operating? A high burn rate could be a sign of a mis-managed company with in-experienced management that are making foolhardy decisions. High overhead costs do not add value to a company.

Fad – Are you investing in a fad or a trend? A trend is semi-permanent and consistent while a fad will fall away fast. A fad lasts for a short period of time and then dissipates.

USP – What is the Unique Selling Proposition? How does the company

GROW RICH

and its product(s) differentiate themselves in their market against their competition?

ROI – Return on Investment is a key factor for Angel Investors and Venture Capitalists. A low Return on Investment is not attractive to investors as they can receive higher returns in other better performing investment vehicles. The discounted cash flow numbers reveal more about your business to an investor than does your charisma and speaking style.

There are businesses that venture capitalists have pumped millions in to only for the business to go bankrupt. Online Grocery Market Delivery service Webvan is an example of a start-up company that received hundreds of millions of dollars of start-up funding but

GROW RICH

went bankrupt. No human being on earth can accurately predict how a business will turn out. There are businesses that have started with $1,000 and have become huge successes by generating millions of dollars per year. The first business I started with my best friend was when I was 21 years old. It was started with $200 and it generated 2.5 million dollars in its first year of operation. External conditions caused us to shut the business down after a few years but it did most certainly generate 2.5 million US Dollars in its first year of operation. What was my total investment? $200. You change your future by taking a chance and investing in a business. A few thousand dollars is really nothing in the scheme of things but if the business takes off, your few thousands of dollars

GROW RICH

can become millions of dollars, as early investors in Amazon stock realized. The angel investors and venture capitalists figure if they throw enough money at businesses, something will become successful. They are not always wrong. If you do keep at it, eventually you will become successful. But it takes effort as well as systematic repetition. If you had an investment opportunity, but the business was not profitable for the first 5 years, would you still invest in it? Amazon is an example of a company that was not profitable for its first 5 years in business but then grew to become a 1 Trillion Dollar company. There is no really no way of accurately predicting future events. All business is chaotic and all business is pure speculation. Luck has played more of a part in success than has preparation. You can

GROW RICH

prepare as much as you want but you cannot control external conditions. You can only react to external conditions as they currently exist. Just as you cannot change external conditions, you cannot change perceptions. You can spend hundreds of millions of dollars and you still will not be able to change everyone's perception. You may be able to change some people's perception but the cost of doing so may be so high that is bankrupts your business. Businesses like Quibi spent billions of dollars only to discover that they could not change perceptions. External conditions dictate the business environment and allow for our reaction. An investment opportunity from a start-up company is an opportunity to participate in the creation of new wealth and an Active Revenue Channel (ARC) for your investment

GROW RICH

portfolio. Investment is either hit or miss. You either become successful or your fail. You can save time and money by investing in a new business start-up rather than attempting to re-invent the wheel. How do you know if you will succeed in your investment in a new business? You don't. You can only hope for success but as long as you study the numbers before investing, you are able to somewhat accurately predict the short term outcome (but not long term outcomes since they depend on external conditions). Let us take the example of a business investor that decides to invest in 5 gas stations. A smart move on the investor's part as gasoline prices are steadily rising. In the short term, the investor is able to predict the short term outcomes. Unfortunately for the business investor that invested in the 5

GROW RICH

gas stations, new Environmental Protection Agency regulations require the gas stations to replace the underground gasoline tanks to prevent leakage. The business investor invested 2 million dollars for a majority share in 5 gas stations but now has to spend 6 million dollars replacing the underground tanks, causing the business investor to declare bankruptcy. In the short term, the business investor was able to predict the short term outcome of achieving healthy profits but was not able to control the External Conditions that would affect his business investment in the long term. This is why business is dynamic rather than static. New problems arise rather than the repetition of old problems. The new problems are caused by external conditions and it is up to the business to

GROW RICH

react to them without having any
knowledge of their effects in the long
term. It is for this reason that all
business investments are pure
speculation like betting red or black in a
casino. The numbers (Balance Sheet,
Profit and Loss Statement, etc) can only
provide you with comfort in the short
term but cannot shield you from external
conditions in the long term. An external
condition that you cannot control is the
entry of competitors in to that industry
you have invested in. Another external
condition is technology. Brick and
mortar stores were alarmed at their drop
in sales which was in direct correlation
to the rise of e-commerce. The music
companies could not control the external
condition of music changing from CD's
to digital MP3's. Disruption is an
external condition that cannot be

predicted in the short term but its effects and impact are realized in the long term. These were just a few examples of external conditions that are known of but there are many external conditions that are not readily seeable. They have to be discovered in the course of business. Angel investors and venture capitalists are by no means perfect and they do make many mistakes. As an angel investor or venture capitalist, you will also make mistakes, but the mistakes should be learning lessons that can be applied to your next investment. It takes courage to hand money over to a start-up company with the hope that they will become successful. Many successful investors in start-up companies tend to take an active role and interest in the daily, monthly, and yearly operations of that company. They want to watch over

GROW RICH

their investment and they are right for doing it. If a Venture Capitalist or Angel Investor views a business investment as being viable and attractive but are un-sure of the management team, the investor(s) may seek to take a majority share and to install their own CEO and Board of Directors, in order to ensure the company is being run in a way that they are comfortable with. If you were to invest $50,000 or $500,000, wouldn't you want to have control over the direction of the company (even indirectly)? Many venture capitalists and angel investors do just that in order to guarantee that they will get their money back. They are more aware than anyone that all investments are speculation and they want to make sure that they are able to get their investment back. If you had to attempt to re-create a business

GROW RICH

you were to invest in, it would be prohibitively expensive and time consuming. That time is better spent on finding potential billion dollar companies that are in the seed or start-up stage, and investing in them. They may take time to grow but if one of them does become successful, it will be well worth your effort and time. Before online gaming became mainstream, a certain start-up founder approached a venture capitalist with a business plan to start an online gaming company. The venture capitalist shrugged it off and a short time later, online gaming became globally popular and lucrative. The venture capitalist decided to build his own online game but had no specialization or experience in the field. The venture capitalist created a game that never took off, never achieved success, and

GROW RICH

he had the pleasure of wasting millions of dollars to re-invent the wheel. The game failed and the venture capitalist went on to greener pastures in no time. The point of the story is that you should not attempt to re-invent the wheel and fail, as the venture capitalist turned game builder discovered the hard way (and through considerable loss). The same way that money is leveraged to achieve results and profits, skilled people and specialists have to be leveraged to achieve results. But you cannot hire specialists that know more than you and expect to tell them what to do. The specialists should, with all their expertise, be telling you what to do. That is what you are paying them and that is why you hired them. They should be guiding and moving the process forward using your investment to achieve

GROW RICH

results. Investing in a business is a smart way to leapfrog forward in time and to achieve greater results by leveraging specialists to achieve them. Your money and management should be the catalyst and glue that provides the momentum to achieve business profits. As long as you are willing to put in the time and effort to discover start-up companies, you will have a large pool of companies to make offers to. You have to spend most of your time searching in order to find start-ups that are worthy of your time and investment. Don't re-invent the wheel by attempting to re-create their efforts. Invest in start-up companies and reap the benefits from your astute investing. Businesses are developed naturally over time and they cannot be forced because sometimes external conditions do not allow for

GROW RICH

success. Timing is an external condition that you cannot control but you can react to. Angel investors and venture capitalists are interested in only investing businesses that are the first in their category giving them First Mover Advantage. There are many instances of the first mover creating a category but then losing their position to a Me-Too competitor that was able to offer a better version of the same product. Let us look at the electric car market. In the United States, a brand name electric automobile costs $40,000 to purchase. That same electric car (with fewer innovations) is being manufactured in China and sold in China for $7,000. How long can electric cars be sold for $40,000 by that First Mover before lower priced competitors steal its market share? The First Mover created the

GROW RICH

market and then me-too competitors
came with a less expensive version.
Automobiles are a commodity because
transportation is an essential element in
the function of society. Brands like
Disney do not have the same problem
because they are providing a uniquely
branded service that cannot be copied
or re-produced. It is not a widget to
manufacture. Unique brands that have
built up value in their intellectual
property cannot be copied because they
are able to provide something unique.
Since humans are brand buyers, they
tend to be attracted to brands that have
a unique selling proposition. Even a me-
too brand can become successful
eventually if they are able to differentiate
their brand from their competitors. Brand
differentiation comes through having a
unique selling proposition as well as

GROW RICH

having unique attributes such as "the
fastest", "the longest lasting", or "the
most durable". Caterpillar is an example
of a brand that has unique attributes and
unique branding despite it selling
construction equipment. People fall in
love with a brand and the product or
service is the brand as much as the
brand literally means the product or
service. It may not seem the same but in
the mind of the consumer, the brand
and the product or service are inter-
changeable in meaning. People don't
drink XYZ soft drink because it tastes
good, they are drinking the brand. The
brand is the promise of consistency and
it is a contract between the company
and the end user. The brand is an
assurance of a standard of quality and it
is the representation of the values of
that company. When a brand does not

GROW RICH

exist, it is known as a generic brand. Without a brand, it is a commodity like oranges or rice. When rice was packaged and a picture of a human was put on the package with a brand name, the company doing so was able to charge a premium price for their product. Why were they able to charge a premium (higher) price and not lose sales? Because it was now a recognizable brand with a recognizable brand name. If you are an angel investor or venture capitalist, you cannot expect to be offered a large share of a known brand name for pennies on the dollar. A start-up company has not proven itself through sales revenue and is in need of growth and direction. A large portion of a start-up company can be acquired, 30 percent or more, for small sums of money because the business seeking

GROW RICH

capital is not yet a well-known brand name. A well-known brand name would seek large sums of money for investment because their intellectual property has value whereas a start-up company has not yet developed their brand name. Start-ups depend on cash injections and even a small investment by you can capture a large share of their company stock. It is not a safe investment in comparison to real estate, but it will yield much more than 8 percent or 10 percent return on your investment. Investing in business is rather hit or miss and it is a simple fact that the majority of businesses fail after their first year in operation. The business may be focused around one product or service and future external conditions may cause that business to shut down or change operations. There

GROW RICH

may be other external conditions that can affect your business investment including (but not limited to):

Change In Buying Habits – Buyers can and do change their buying habits according to various factors including supply and demand as well as price.

Timing – You can have a great business idea that is well executed but the timing for market entry was too early or too late.

Negative Press – Negative press can hurt the value of a business and it has in some cases caused business to shut down.

Logistics – Getting your raw materials or goods depends on transportation services. Supply chain disruptions are

common in business and can result in a
business shutting down.

In-consistent Quality – Customers
demand a standard level of quality and
the brand is the contract that guarantees
that service. An inconsistent level of
quality can result in a high attrition (loss)
rate of customers. Batch production has
more in-consistency versus lean
manufacturing which tends to have
lower errors.

Overhead Costs

Overhead costs should be reduced to a
bare minimum. You don't need a
physical office to have a company. You
don't need to pay thousands of dollars a
month for mobile phones for employees
and you don't need a company chef.
You don't need a company driver and

GROW RICH

you don't need to fly first class. What you need is to run a tight ship. What you need is budgeting. If you are able to budget, you will not only not overspend, but you will also be able to save money that could be used at a later date. Spending $7,000 or $2,000 a month for a physical office is frivolous. Oil Billionaire J Paul Getty signed most of his deals on the hood of his Model T Ford. Do you want to do business or do you want to look good and impress others? Is your goal revenue generation or looking good in front of others? Hopefully, your goal is revenue generation. If you are not able to control your costs, it doesn't make any difference how much revenue you can generate. You have to control your costs and the first place to start is overhead. Does it matter if your office is in San

GROW RICH

Francisco or Toledo? You do not have to have a physical location to conduct business. You can conduct business wherever you are standing. People are conducting business with you, not with your office. If you want to impress a business client, take them out to lunch. It will cost less than paying $5,000 for office space that is rarely or never visited by customers. If you are a retail business or you have invested in a retail business, a storefront (brick and mortar or online) is required for conducting business. Even that model is up for debate, as financial institutions switch from a brick and mortar presence to a purely online presence. Virtual organizations are becoming the norm rather than the exception. In a virtual organization, there is no physical location and every employee or

GROW RICH

independent contractor is in a separate location. A consulting company, may choose to not have any physical location and to have thousands of independent contractors selling their services in separate locations. They do not have to show up to any office and check in at 9am and check out at 5pm. They can work from anywhere, they do not waste time on commuting, and they video conferencing software like Zoom or Skype to communicate. Businesses are moving towards the virtual organization model because of the enormous reduction in costs that the virtual organization model provides. A corporate campus has thousands of employess on-site working. A dentist is on-site so that the employees don't leave and multiple restaurants are on site so that the employees don't leave.

GROW RICH

Add in security costs, utilities costs, and rising real estate costs, and the overhead expenses can be very costly for a company maintaining a physical location. Overhead costs do not add value to the customer proposition and they do not add value to products or services. From a purely financial point of view, overhead costs are frivolous and are a waste. It is money that is irretrievably gone and the expenditure did not create any more value for your customers. If you do not have to have a physical location, then do not waste money having one. A business can be run from home just as well as it can be run from an office. What is an office? 4 walls, a door, desk, chair, computer, filing cabinet, and telephone. An office doesn't make better employees. The employees bring value to an office.

GROW RICH

Managing Your Business Investment

Any sane individual that invests in a company will seek to manage over their investment through various means. The investor as an Angel Investor or Venture Capitalist will not only want frequent monthly and/or quarterly reporting, but they will also want a minority or majority position on the Board of Directors of your company. If you are a start-up company that does not need venture capital, then do not seek it out. Another owner in your company means more voices on your Board of Directors. It means oversight and auditing of your numbers and your business practices. If you are investing in a company, it is only logical that you will seek to manage over that investment personally (or through an intermediary). You should receive a

GROW RICH

sizeable share of a company that you invest in so that it is worth your time to give attention to it. Taking a 5 percent stake in a company for your $50,000 investment is not worth it, because the return on investment will not justify the investment. Every business is not destined to become a billion dollar company or even a multi-million dollar company. Micro-investments can be made in micro-businesses, but the returns may not justify your time and investment. If you made a $50,000 investment for 30 percent of a company, it would be worth your time and money to look over your investment and to keep in constant contact with the remaining shareholders in order to discuss the direction of the company. One of the most useful methods for having insight in to the operations of a

GROW RICH

business you have invested in is to make frequent visits to that business. You can use Management By Walking Around (MBWA) to view the business in its daily operations in order to make recommendations to that business that would reduce their expenses, increase their sales, optimize their floor plans, increase efficiency, and boost productivity. You can access their accounting reports and view the numbers. You can require weekly or monthly reporting from the Board of Directors. You can increase the value of your investment by having an active say in its operations. If you buy 100 or 10000 high priced shares in a multi-billion dollar public company, you can't show up to their corporate office or to their factory and act like you are of importance or holding any official

GROW RICH

position. They would probably laugh as you roll up outside their corporate factory and demand to be obeyed because you bought 100 or 10000 high priced shares in their multi-billion dollar public company. When you invest in a start-up company and you acquire a sizeable share such as 30 percent or more, then you are given a seat on the Board of Directors, and you are able to make recommendations and to demand that your input be accepted. This is why a Venture Capitalist with 50 million dollars seeks out start-up companies. Couldn't that venture capitalist go and buy 100000 shares of a multi-billion dollar tech company? Sure they could. Then they would own .003 percent of the shares of that company. That wouldn't even get them an invitation to that company's Christmas dinner much

GROW RICH

less give them any say in the operation of that company. The venture capitalists and angel investors want to get in on the ground floor and be there from day one so that they could realize the possible enormous returns the capital markets will award that company in the future. The best way to manage over your investment In a start-up business is to put in time and visit that business often. This will provide you with empirical evidence of issues the company. No one seeking money approaches a venture capitalist or angel investor, preaching about the problems or pitfalls of a business. Everyone wants to look good and no one wants to look bad. It is up to you to discover the problems that the business is facing by viewing the numbers. The numbers are a tall tale sign of the problems the business is

GROW RICH

facing and the numbers will provide you with the information you need to make an informed business investment decision. People seeking money sweep problems under the rug in order to highlight the advantages and benefits of investing in a certain business. Although investing in a business is an art rather than a science, it does depend on the numbers to reveal the true image. The numbers will allow you to understand if the debt the company has acquired was good or bad debt. The numbers will reveal if the company has a low turnover by the amount of un-sold product it is holding in a warehouse. The numbers will reveal if the executives or management are pilfering the company. The numbers will tell you if the corporate buyer is over-paying for routine services. The numbers will reveal if the company buyer is stealing money and taking kickbacks for buying from over-charging greedy suppliers. The numbers will reveal how much each employee is generating in income on average per year. The numbers reveal the true Cost of Goods Sold and the numbers reveal the cost of customer acquisition. The numbers will reveal if there is a lack of demand for the company's product(s). The numbers reveal everything about an investment, which is why an accountant is the most important specialist that you could receive consulting from before you invest in a business. As the old adage goes "If the numbers don't add up, it doesn't make sense". A trained accountant can easily find problems in the numbers and could provide advice that will prevent you from making bad decisions. If you want to invest in a

GROW RICH

business and that business owner is not willing to share the numbers with you, then you should avoid doing business with such a person.

Budgeting

Even if your Active Revenue Channels generate 100 million dollars per year, you can still spend it frivolously if you do not budget. Every business, as well as every home, has to operate on a budget. If you are not cautious in your expenses you will see your profits wasted on activities that do no increase your sales or add value to the customer. You have to apply a budget and you have to stick to that budget to prevent financial mis-management. If you are investing in a business that is a call center, is it important where they are located? Do they have to be located in a

GROW RICH

glitzy commercial office space that costs $50,000 per month or will a $2,000 per month warehouse suffice? Does every employee need a mobile phone that is paid for by the business? Does a business executive need to fly first class or will economy class be sufficient? Are the company executives holding expensive non-value adding company parties that add to the burn rate? Is the company pool table essential for transacting business? Is it the company's responsibility to spend $15,000 per month on stocking the fridge and providing free snacks? Are there too many executives in a company paying themselves high salaries? Is there a need to buy XYZ raw material and pay exorbitant storage fees to store it for 6 months in order to manufacture finished goods today? Is it necessary to spend money on manufacturing when the business inventory is filled with un-sold goods? There are many areas in a business in which costs can be cut without sacrificing quality. Efficiency depends on reducing the waste in order to increase productivity (rate of output). Major businesses seek to invest in technology such as robotics to reduce costs while raising revenue. It should be the goal of all businesses to seek ways to reduce costs while increasing revenue through sales.

Marketing

Marketing is communication that creates brand awareness for your company. It makes the job of the sales person easier. It is easier to cold call decision makers when your brand is well known. An unknown brand has to go through

GROW RICH

the steps of educating their customer about their brand and its unique attributes. Marketing was viewed as advertising in the 1960's and these two terms were practically and functionally identical. Advertising is one element of marketing. It is important that you understand the various forms of marketing so that you are able to benefit from them. The types of Marketing include but are not limited to:

Affiliate Marketing – Paid Referrals to independent online marketers.

Cause Marketing – Representing the values of a cause (protect the environment) in your communications.

Chat Marketing – Live Chats that are hosted online with the purpose of interacting with potential or current customers.

Demo Marketing – Public demonstrations of the product or service at a location that has large amounts of foot traffic.

Direct Mail Marketing – Bulk Mail

Email Marketing – Bulk Email sent using an email list (usually a spreadsheet).

Endorsement Marketing – Paid Influencers that feature your product or service in return for payment.

Gift Marketing – Promotional gifts sent to key decision makers in corporations.

Guerrilla Marketing – Unorthodox style of marketing that uses stickers, wall posters, graffiti, and other means to broadcast a message.

In-Flight Marketing – Advertisements inside airline magazines or in airplanes.

Mobile Marketing – Bulk SMS/Text that is sent to mobile phones of potential or current customers.

Outdoor Marketing – Billboards and bus stop advertisements.

Radio Marketing – Short Radio Ads featured before and after TV shows.

Referral Marketing – Pay customers a commission for referrals.

Research Marketing – Research marketing is the use of surveys to discover customer buying habits. Questions are posed to potential customers about various products or

GROW RICH

services. The answers are analyzed and recommendations are made based on that information.

Social Media Marketing - Online

Television Marketing – TV Ads

Trade Show Marketing – Exhibitions are an important method for marketing your products and services to global buyers.

Transit Marketing – Advertisements on or inside moving vehicles including busses, trains, cars, and other transportation.

Viral Marketing – Word of Mouth

Voice Marketing – Podcasts, sound clips, and audio streams.

GROW RICH

Promotional Marketing - Promotional marketing has many forms and they include (but are not limited to):

Coupons – Coupons are a popular way of attracting bargain buyers seeking discounts.

Free Stuff – People love getting promotional items and companies give away millions of branded pens, t-shirts, stickers, bags, and various gifts to potential and current customers each year. Trade shows are a popular location that companies use to give away promotional items.

Free Trial – Free trials are offered to use the product or service for free and to pay if they are satisfied.

Loyalty Programs – Loyalty cards and Member ID numbers are issued to each

GROW RICH

customer, allowing them to earn points and get discounts in the future. Loyalty programs have been used successfully by airlines as well as grocery supermarket chains to understand the buying trends among customers and to create customer loyalty.

Giveaways – Contests or sweepstakes excite potential and current customers. Giveaways entice potential customers to enter in order to win an item. The potential customers provide the business with their information, allowing that business to market and sell to those potential customers at a future date.

Sales

There are many forms of marketing, but the ultimate goal of marketing is the creation of sales. Marketing makes your

GROW RICH

job easier and makes the sales process smoother. Just as it is important for you to have understanding of Marketing, it is important for you to understand the various forms of Selling and they include (but are not limited to):

Business Development – Corporate partnerships with companies that agree to sell your products/services.

Channel Sales – Finding retail resellers to sell your products/services to end users. Channel Sales is a very powerful sales method because it leverages the already existing network of retailer to re-sell your products and services. Sales can increase exponentially using channel sales.

GROW RICH

Demo Sales – Sales from a booth that is publicly demonstrating a product or service.

Direct Sales – Making cold or warm calls to potential customers with the purpose of making them a customer. Also known as Telemarketing or Outbound Sales.

Door to Door Sales – The oldest form of selling is door to door sales. It was direct selling before there was phone direct sales. Many major businesses grew through targeted door to door sales to homes and businesses.

E-Commerce Sales – Sales generated from an online store such as selling on Amazon.

Infomercials – Effective television selling method that uses long advertisements, 30 to 40 minutes in length, to generate responses from potential customers, leading to an inbound phone call sale.

You have to understand the 4 types of buyers and what motivates them to purchase.

Convenience Buyer – The convenience buyer purchases a product or service because of the purchasing ease. They are motivated by the ease of purchasing the product as a solution, rather than by the product itself. A buyer of online food delivery services is most likely a convenience buyer. A buyer of online groceries is most likely a convenience buyer.

Price Buyer – The price buyer is motivated by hunting for bargains and

GROW RICH

finding the lowest price possible. Many consumer electronics companies started out by appealing to price buyers, by undercutting their competitors on price. A buyer of a Low Cost Budget Airline ticket is most likely a price buyer. A buyer that purchases food at the 99 Cents Store is most likely a Price Buyer.

Brand Buyer – The brand buyer is motivated by status and symbols that project an image for its user. The brand buyer is not motivated by price or convenience, and will pay a premium price and experience in-convenience (wait in lines) in order to acquire the desired product or service. A buyer of an Apple iPhone is most likely a Brand Buyer.

Value Buyer – The value buyer is motivated by receiving the most value

GROW RICH

for the least amount paid. They are interested in receiving the greatest value for the purchase they are making. A buyer of a Toyota automobile is most likely a Value Buyer.

Knowing what motivates your customers make the job of selling to them much easier. Selling to your customers is the lifeline of your company. Every department should exist to support the Sales department and their selling efforts. Sales define a company's Profit and Loss statement and they result in a healthy Balance Sheet. Sales efforts should define all of the operations of a company and should lead the company's other departments. If you are afraid of selling, then you must hire people that can sell for you. Everything you do is a sales job. In investing, you are selling a business on why they should take your investment rather than that of your competitor. When you buy an owner financed home, you are selling the Seller as to the reasons that they should sell the house to you. It doesn't feel like Sales and it doesn't necessarily have to. All Revenue Generation occurs by Sales and it is by far the most important function of your company and it is the function in which you should invest the most time and effort. Sales fuels human resources and sales fuel the dollars that the marketing department uses to communicate the brand. It is important to understand the steps involved in direct selling. As CEO, you may tell yourself that you are not a Salesperson, but you will be surprised to find out that the CEO's of companies are the top salesperson in their

GROW RICH

organization because they are out meeting with other CEO's and forming alliances. Even the CEO is a salesperson because they are selling the brand values of that organization to a wider audience. Everything comes down to sales and there are many instances of organizations shutting down because of one or two major sales accounts being lost. A major shipbuilder that loses out on a five hundred million dollar order could risk having to downsize or shut down. A major commercial airplane manufacturer that loses a key order could end up having to downsize. Lost sales has huge consequences for a company and those consequences can include bankruptcy, downsizing, closing departments, and scaling operations. Lost sales through customer switching or lost sales through

GROW RICH

high attrition, can break a business and cause it to re-organize. Each sales call does cost you time and money, which is why you should prepare beforehand before contacting a potential customer. What it is that you want to say? What do you want the result of this phone call to be? Do you want to move the forward one step closer to a sale on this call or are you are seeking to get the customer to pay on this call? If you plan beforehand the flow of the call and rehearse it in your mind or on paper, you will be better able to achieve the results you are seeking. Picture yourself in your mind closing the call with success and reaching the outcome you are seeking. Understand your motives before making the call and you will be able to easily understand the direction the call should be going in.

GROW RICH

Sales Steps

Introduction – Make a simple introduction and introduce your company and yourself.

Discover Decision maker(s) – You have to discover the names of the key decision maker(s) that are responsible for purchasing what you are selling.

Qualifications – How much does the buyer buy per year? What problems are they facing that you could provide a solution for? Are they the sole decision-maker?

In Person/Online/Phone Presentation – Give a presentation on the product or service you are selling. Include a proposal if necessary.

GROW RICH

Handling Objections – Answer any questions they have. Each question is a concern in the form of a question. Handle their concerns by answering their questions. An objection is really a request for more information on the part of the buyer. Inability to properly handle objections from a potential customer could result in you losing the sale and losing the customer permanently.

Closing – You have to ask for their business and for them to buy from you. There are various ways to close a sale and they include writing up the order, the pros and cons comparison, and asking for their business.

Writing Up The Order is as simple as filling out the printed or online order form that completes the sale and asking questions from the customer to fill in the

GROW RICH

fields to complete the order. Ask them how they would like to pay and lead them to payment. Writing Up The Order is a linear closing technique that leads the buyer from introduction to the close. A bookseller in a bookstore asks what the customer wants, provides them with a solution, and then leads them to the cash register. It is a linear closing technique. Pros and Cons Comparison is a very simple yet effective closing technique whereby you use a piece of paper or image to convey the pros (positives) about buying your product or service versus the cons (negatives) about buying your product or service. The Pros and Cons Comparison is a powerful closing technique that provides a visual to the customer and better helps them understand the benefits of buying your product or service. Asking

GROW RICH

For Their Business is a closing technique that has the Seller ask the Buyer to buy from them based on the presentation you have delivered. It is a logical and practical close that uses a straightforward statement to close the sale.

Conditions

Conditions affect your sale and they can prevent you from moving forward in your sale. Sales conditions are not an objection or a request for more information about your products or services. Conditions that prevent the sale must be recorded by the seller so that the seller can re-visit the buyer when the condition(s) have passed. The first condition is if all the decision makers are not present to make a decision together. Another condition is

GROW RICH

that the decision to purchase may be
made by a group of individuals that
meet 3 times per year and their next
meeting is 3 months away, causing you
to have to delay the sale for 3 months.
Another condition is that their current
budget is not enough to purchase your
product. There are a myriad of
conditions that affect sales and prevent
you from moving forward. A condition is
different than an objection, which is just
a request for more information. A
condition is a real reason why the sale
cannot move forward currently. Whether
you personally sell or you have
salespersons working for you, it is
important to have understanding of
sales so that it can help increase your
revenue. No product sells itself except a
commodity like gasoline. Gasoline sells
itself because an automobile or a

GROW RICH

motorcycle cannot work without it.
Because gasoline is a commodity, it
cannot be branded like a shoe company
brand. Electricity is a utility (electricity
can be considered a commodity) and it
therefore cannot be branded like a
luxury men's clothing brand. A brand
does not just sell itself. Whether if it is a
product or service, it has to be sold.
Even if you are IBM or Honda or
Caterpillar or Samsung, the
salespersons sell their products (or
services) in a pro-active (rather than
passive) manner. Nothing just sells
itself. Everything has to be sold and
salespersons are a company's most
important corporate asset because they
are the driver of its revenue growth.
Without sales, a company has nothing.
It is not enough to exist as a company.
A company has to drive sales resulting

GROW RICH

in income generation. Income
generation is the purpose of sales and
increasing sales volume will allow a
business to grow.

Public Relations

Public relations is the science of
shaping and molding public perception.
You cannot change the perception of
everyone but you can change the
perception of some people. There are
various tools that are used in public
relations to shape the perceptions of
others. One of the most important tools
for reaching a mass audience and
shaping perception is a Press Release.
A Press Release is an advertisement in
the form of a news style article. To the
untrained eye, it is a news article. To the
public relations professional, it is a tool
for shaping public perception. A press

GROW RICH

release is written in an inverted pyramid format, with the most important part being at the top and the least important parts being at the bottom. An effective press release has a theme, quotes from individuals (business executive), and is informative as news should be. It is the creation of news for the purpose of Image Projection. Image Projection is the use of communication to create a favorable image towards a person or business. Why is this beneficial to a business? Businesses depend on creating a positive image that can assist them create a loyal customer base. Negative reputations hurt business sales in the short term but also hurt their chances of creating a loyal customer base in the long term. Public Relations uses emotional, intellectual, scientific, and biological appeals to manipulate

GROW RICH

perceptions. Public relations, like all well-crafted news, features informative reporting as well as seeking to shape a narrative. The narrative is shaped by the creation of the news story and a press release is drafted to convey that narrative in the form of a news article. The narrative must be planned in order to arrive at a theme and consequently the story. The story becomes the news article, written in the point of view of a reporter that is reporting on the news in an un-biased format. The press release is drafted and edited and prepared to be sent out to multiple newspapers, radio stations, news websites, media outlets, an independent news desks. The Press Release allows you to reach a mass buying audience with the hopes of shaping their perception in regards to your company's products or services.

GROW RICH

Sample Press Release

(DATE) – Startup company XYZ announced on Tuesday that they will be releasing their new ABC product next fall. XYZ's ABC product has received numerous awards for its work on creating jobs in economically distressed communities. The ABC product created a wave among the youth, becoming a near mainstream trend selling $50,000 in their first day. XYZ VP of Affairs said "We are thrilled with the outpour of support for ABC and we are encouraged by the results we are seeing in these communities. XYZ strives to better the lives of everyone especially members of our community". The ABC product will be released in the first month of fall. For more information about XYZ company visit www.yourdomainname.com.

GROW RICH

The Purpose

If you are seeking to attract investors, attract businesses to invest in, make buying owner financed properties easier, then you have to have a positive image in the business community. Public relations shapes that public image and makes your business dealings smoother and easier. A negative image would make your business dealings more difficult. This is why companies are heavily invested in public relations. Even as an angel investor or venture capitalist, public relations affects you. Positive public relations can attract new start-ups to your business. Positive public relations can make owner financed property sellers aware of your request to buy homes. The news article could even be

GROW RICH

written to make it seem that you are saving owner financed properties by buying them. XYZ buys owner financed homes to save homeowners from foreclosure. A positive public image acts as a force multiplier for your business and boosts your standing in the community. It is important to understand that all news is generated and created. All news. Your news is no different than anyone else's news. It is just news. You have to generate news to push a positive image of your business so that it is easier for you to transact any type of business, whether if you are buying an owner financed home or if you are investing in a business. Public relations work and it helps to create momentum for your business dealings. Once the press release has been written, it has to be submitted to various news outlets

GROW RICH

and it is of vital importance to personally contact each of the news outlets that received your press release. By speaking personally with each reporter, you raise your chances of having your press release printed and you raise your chances of having the reporter interview you for quotes they will use in that article. You have to be accustomed to maintaining regular communications with various reporters and harvesting the relationships so that they can be leveraged at a future date. A positive image can build up your reputation and open doors for your company that would have been closed without it. One press release will not achieve the results you are seeking. It is important to use a series of press releases, usually three press releases. A series of press releases sent out every 2 weeks will

GROW RICH

achieve results. Digital press conferences can also be held using video conferencing apps such as Zoom. Online press conferences are press conferences in which all of the participants are in separate locations. Press are invited to ask questions and a public relations specialist answers questions on behalf of their organization. Whether if you use press releases or online press conferences, the point is to convey your message to reporters who will in turn relay your message(s) to a larger audience. It is vital to maintain a list or database of public relations contacts that you have developed over time. This will make the job of sending out new press releases and contacting news reporters much easier. Reporters need news and it is your goal to create news to feed them.

GROW RICH

Your news will seek to portray a positive image of your company and to project an image. Public relations seeks to shape a narrative and to mold public perception in regards to your products/service or company. You have to generate the news to help your business differentiate itself among competitors. News is generated and pushed to reporters who in turn have it published with their respective news outlets. Either you are generating your own news are you are reading news that was generated for you by others. Either way, someone has to generate the news. Your business should generate its own news regarding its operations. As a business it is your duty to shape the news so that it helps your company achieve higher profits.

GROW RICH

Investing To Win

The only way to win is to play the game.
You have to play the game to win
because there is nothing to be gained
by not playing. Whether if you are
investing in owner financed homes,
buying gold, or investing in a start-up
business, you have to play the game to
win. Negative people that tell you that
you can't do something are probably
afraid that you will. They project their
own insecurities on to you as a way to
make themselves feel powerful. They
can't do it, so you can't do it, is the false
logic they employ. When you make a
decision to win, there should be nothing
to stop you. Everything else becomes a
distraction that should be avoided and
the only thing that does matter is your
success. Success cannot be wished in

GROW RICH

to existence. It depends on your work ethic and your will (internal drive) to win. There is no evidence that you will become successful if you have a positive attitude but there is huge evidence to support the belief that you will be un-successful if you are negative. There is nothing to be gained from naysayers but there is much to be learned from positive successful people. If you could view a list of 100 successful people and choose their most important quality, what do you think it would be? Will. Having the internal drive to keep moving forward in the face of difficulty and to never quit. No matter how many setbacks you experience, you have to keep moving forward in order to progress. Setbacks are learning experiences that you can grow from. Setbacks are expensive knowledge that acquired in the course of business. They are also an opportunity to re-direct your efforts and to achieve new results.

Simple Business Accounting

You do not need to be an accountant to understand basic business accounting and bookkeeping. Ultimately, the goal of all your business operations (buying owner financed real estate properties, buying gold, investing in a business, etc) should be the creation of Net Income. Your total revenues minus your total expenses equals your Net Income.

Revenue – Expenses = Net Income

The Balance Sheet equation helps a business understand their true worth (Assets) by adding up the Capital invested by the owner with the Liabilities (Debt).

GROW RICH

Capital + Liabilities = Assets

It is important to understand your cost of goods sold (COGS) in order to arrive at the gross profit.

For example, let us say you bought 1,000 wrenches at the beginning of the month and put them in your inventory. Each wrench cost $2. Then in the middle of the month you bought another 1,000 wrenches at $2 per piece. When the month finishes you have only 1,000 wrenches left at $2 per piece.

Beginning Inventory + Inventory Purchases – Remaining Inventory = Cost of Goods Sold

$2,000 + $2,000 - $2,000 = $2,000

GROW RICH

Gross Profit can be calculated subtracting the Cost of Goods Sold from the Total Sales Income.

Total Sales Income – Cost of Goods Sold = Gross Profit

For example, you sold 1,000 wrenches for $5 per piece giving you a Total Sales Income of $5,000.

$5,000 - $2,000 = $3,000

Gross Profit Margin can be calculated by diving by the Total Sales Income by the Gross Profit.

Gross Profit/Sales = Gross Profit Margin

It is of vital importance to know your Break Even Point and to do that you must subtract the Cost of Goods Sold Per Unit from the Per Unit Sales Price

GROW RICH

and divide that sum by your Fixed
Costs.

**Fixed Costs/(Per Unit Sales Price –
Cost of Goods Sold Per Unit) = Break
Even Point**

For example, your fixed costs (rent,
monthly expenses) for 1 year are
$30,000 a year.

Let us say that you sold each wrench for
$3 and your Cost Goods Sold Per Unit
was $2. That would leave you with $1.

$30000/($3-$2) = 30,000 wrenches. You
would have to sell 30,000 wrenches in
one year in order to break even.

You would have to sell 2,500 wrenches
on a monthly basis in order to break
even. Increasing the price could
increase your profit margin but it could

GROW RICH

reduce sales, depending on the price elasticity of your product or service. Price Elasticity (sensitivity of buyer to price increases or decreases) plays a huge role in determining sales. Toyota sells more cars than Rolls Royce and that is because the sales price that the buyer pays plays a huge role in the decision making process of the value buyer.

Hourly Net Income can be quantified by dividing the Net Income by the Hours Invested (time it took you to create the net income).

Net Income/Hours Invested = Hourly Net Income (Before Taxes and Insurance)

$100,000/1000 hours = $100 per hour

GROW RICH

You generated $100,000 in 1000 hours of work. You generated $100 per hour.

You Can Do It

You have to believe in yourself. You have to become motivated about achieving success. You have to plan to achieve success and you have to take the necessary steps in order to achieve it. No can do it for you. You have to do it and you have to believe in your ability to achieve it. The reason why titans of industry like Getty or Hershey are talked about is because they were able to become very rich (despite having started off poor). They were able to beat the odds through strategy and planning and execution. You too can beat the odds if you are dedicated to winning and you have planned and executed correctly. We are all born poor but

GROW RICH

whether we decide to live poor or die poor is our choice. You too can win and you must tell yourself that you are a winner. You have to focus on business and income generation so that you will acquire the necessary first-hand experience required to win. Everyone has a heartbreak, failure, or setback that they are embittered about. One setback or two or three or four or five, should not discourage you from becoming a success. You have to move from failure to the next investment without becoming discouraged. No one has ever made money by living in the past. You have to live for the present and you will see the results in the future. The seeds of your future success are watered by your actions in the present. Live in the present, not in the past. Your future will be a successful future if you start

GROW RICH

achieving in the present. You can do it
and you can achieve anything that you
set your heart to, but you have to be
consistent. Pessimism has never made
anyone money. Optimism (being
positive) can make you money because
it will provide you with the enthusiasm
required to try new business ventures.
90 percent of all businesses fail in the
first year. Should you hide in a cave and
do nothing because 90 percent of
businesses fail in the first year? Of
course not. Investment is as much trial
and error as it is an art. Despite
investment dealing with numbers,
investing is surely not a science. Some
just get lucky and achieve success
because the conditions allowed for it.
Some fail and have bad luck because
the conditions caused it. All investments
are absolutely speculation but it is

GROW RICH

through speculation (investing in a business or investing in real estate), that you are able to make money. Real Estate is a relatively safe speculation which is why your return on investment will be around 10 percent a year while investing in a business is a riskier speculation that provides much higher rates of return on your investment. You can do it. You too can become successful and you can Grow Rich, by smartly investing in real estate and in businesses. Seek advice from lawyers and accountants, and then move forward with the peace of mind that you have done your Due Diligence. Buy owner financed properties, re-model them, re-finance them, and rent them out to achieve an Active Revenue Channel. Create an Active Revenue Channel by investing in a profitable

GROW RICH

business. In order to Grow Rich, you have to create multiple Active Revenue Channels that are each producing income for you. You have to have motivation about achieving success and you have to keep that level of motivation. If you are not motivated by success, then you should look at the items will motivate you such as owning your dream house. Pick things that will motivate you. If it is family, then understand that you are motivated to achieve success so that you can better the lives of your family members. Whatever your motivation is, let that be the fuel that fires your inner drive to succeed. You can achieve any level of success that you want as long as you are willing to dedicate yourself and your time to achieving it. No one was born successful. Anyone that became

GROW RICH

successful and rich worked very hard to achieve success and they did so by being motivated. If you are motivated, consistent, and capable, you can achieve success by chasing success. Success is not going to chase you. You have to pursue success in business and in investing. You have to be motivated and pro-active. Most of all, you have to be thick-skinned and you have to be able to withstand difficult conditions until they pass. Setbacks and failures are not permanent. You can change your life and you can become more successful through hard work and dedication to your business investments. Whether if you are going to start purchasing owner financed properties or if you are going to invest in start-up businesses, you have to stay motivated to achieve success and you have to be able to deal with a

GROW RICH

myriad of problems, without becoming discouraged. The history of business is littered with successes that started out as business failures. Success is not handed to anyone on a silver platter. Success is earned. Titans of industry like Getty and Hershey became successful after experiencing multiple failures. Failures did not define these great business entrepreneurs, nor have failures defined the lives of other titans of industry. Success defined them and they achieved success despite many failures, because they were able to keep their level of motivation and enthusiasm while moving on to their next venture. You can do it. You can achieve success in your business and real estate investments. You deserve success and you deserve to achieve anything that you set your mind and heart to. Stay

GROW RICH

motivated, keep your enthusiasm, and you will achieve success. You can do it. You can achieve success and you can Grow Rich, as long as you take the steps involved to achieve it. There are no shortcuts or fast routes to success. There is only smart speculation, whether if you are investing in an owner financed real estate property of if you are making an investment in a business.

GROW RICH

Kambiz Mostofizadeh Books (Paperback)
25 Principles of Martial Arts
amazon.com/dp/0983594600

25 Principles of Strategy
amazon.com/dp/1942825129

American Antifa
amazon.com/dp/1942825137

American Bookstore Directory
amazon.com/dp/1942825293

Arctic Black Gold
amazon.com/dp/1937981169

Back to Gold
amazon.com/dp/1942825099

Camping Survival Handbook
amazon.com/dp/1942825021

Economic Collapse Survival Manual
amazon.com/dp/1942825056

Find The Ideal Husband
amazon.com/dp/1937981045

Game Creation Manual
amazon.com/dp/1942825048

History of Aliens
amazon.com/dp/1942825102

Hollywood Talent Agency Directory
amazon.com/dp/1942825285

GROW RICH

Independent Filmmakers Handbook
amazon.com/dp/1942825390

Internet Connected World
amazon.com/dp/1942825064

Karate 360
amazon.com/dp/0983594627

Learning Magic
amazon.com/dp/0983594635

Magic as Science and Religion
amazon.com/dp/1937981088

Make Racists Afraid Again
amazon.com/dp/1942825145

Mikazuki Jujitsu Manual
amazon.com/dp/0615473113

Mikazuki Political Science Manual
amazon.com/dp/1937981509

MMA Dictionary
amazon.com/dp/1942825161

Musashi Cop
amazon.com/dp/1942825412

Musashi Cop and the Port Gang
amazon.com/dp/1942825420

Mythology Dictionary
amazon.com/dp/194282517X

Native Americana

GROW RICH

amazon.com/dp/1942825072

Ninja Style
amazon.com/dp/1942825153

Ouija Board Enigma
amazon.com/dp/1942825110

Political Advertising Manual
amazon.com/dp/0983594643

Quotes Gone Wild
amazon.com/dp/099102852X

Saba Squirrel and the Golden Acorn
amazon.com/dp/1942825404

Secrets of Making Money
amazon.com/dp/0991028597

Shinzen Karate
amazon.com/dp/0991028589

Small Arms & Deep Pockets
amazon.com/dp/193798110X

Shogun X the Last Immortal
amazon.com/dp/0991028511

The Bribe Vibe
amazon.com/dp/1937981142

Triggering Everyone
amazon.com/dp/B08KH2K6WV

Van Carlton Detective Agency
amazon.com/dp/0991028503